FLORIDA TEST PREP

FAST Practice Test Book

Star Reading

Grade 2

ISBN 9798376729328

TEST MASTER PRESS

CONTENTS

INTRODUCTION
For Parents, Teachers, and Tutors

About the New Florida Assessment of Student Thinking (F.A.S.T.)

Beginning in the 2022-2023 school year, students in Florida will take the Florida Assessment of Student Thinking (F.A.S.T.). This is a Progress Monitoring System that involves taking tests throughout the school year to show current level and progress. Students in Grade 2 will take the STAR Reading test produced by Renaissance Learning. The tests are taken three times throughout the year. This practice test book will prepare students for the STAR Reading tests.

About Florida's New English Language Arts Standards

Student learning and assessment in Florida is based on the skills listed in the new Benchmarks for Excellent Student Thinking, or B.E.S.T. The reading standards are divided into three areas: Reading Prose and Poetry, Reading Informational Text, and Reading Across Genres. The STAR Reading tests also cover the skills in the Vocabulary section of the standards. This practice test book covers all the reading and vocabulary skills assessed on the test. The answer key at the back of the book includes the skill assessed by each question.

About the Star Reading Tests

The Star Reading tests assess reading skills by having students answer multiple-choice questions with three answer choices. Many of the questions include a short passage, while others are stand-alone. Each test contains 34 questions. Stand-alone questions should be answered within 1 minute and passage-based questions should be answered within 2 minutes.

Taking the Practice Tests

This book contains four practice tests similar to the real Star Reading tests. To cover all the skills well, each practice test contains 36 questions. The tests in this book have been divided into three sections of 12 questions each. This allows students to have ongoing practice, and for review and feedback between sessions. A complete test can also be practiced by taking all 3 sessions in a row.

Practice Test 1

Session 1

Instructions

Read each question carefully.

Each question has three answer choices.

Fill in the circle for the correct answer.

---

1   Welcome to the world of animals! Animals come in all shapes, sizes, and colors. Some animals live in the sky, some live in the ocean, and some even live underground! Some have big teeth or horns to help them hunt. Each animal is unique and special.

What is the text meant to do?

① inform

② entertain

③ persuade

2   The sun shone like a blazing fire in the sky.

What does this simile show about the sun?

① It is near.

② It is bright.

③ It is dangerous.

3   I learned how to ride a bike with the help of my dad. He was very patient. I fell over again and again, but he told me to keep trying. I was so proud when I finally did it.

Which word tells what the dad is like?

①   help

②   patient

③   proud

4   The sun is shining bright,
It's a beautiful day,
I can play with my kite,
And run around and play.

What is the rhyme pattern?

①   AABB

②   ABAB

③   ABCB

5   Simon arrived at school very _____.

Which word completes the sentence?

①   bus

②   class

③   early

6   Emily loved to play with her dolls. One day, she saw a little girl who didn't have any toys. Emily offered to share her dolls with the little girl. They played together happily. The little girl thanked Emily for her kindness.

What is the story about?

①   working hard

②   sharing with others

③   asking for help

7   The castle was <u>massive</u>. It towered above everything else in the town.

What does the word *massive* mean?

①   very costly

②   very big

③   very nice

8   Rain is very important. It helps to keep the air clean. It also provides water for plants and animals. Rain can also be a lot of fun to play in! Some people enjoy jumping in puddles or watching a thunderstorm. Rain is also needed to grow food.

Which detail explains why rain is very important?

①   It is fun to play in.

②   People like jumping in puddles.

③   It is needed to grow food.

9   My name is Emily. I love to draw. I draw pictures of my friends. I love drawing animals too. I think I'm very good at it.

What is the text about?

①   Emily's hobby

②   Emily's family

③   Emily's pets

10   Wade was <u>careless</u> with his things.

What is the base word of *careless*?

①   car

②   care

③   less

11   The Eiffel Tower is in Paris, France. It was built in 1889. It stands at 324 meters tall. The tower has three levels that are open to the public. Tourists can enjoy amazing views of Paris.

Where is the Eiffel Tower located?

① Rome

② Paris

③ Berlin

12   The art in a text is below.

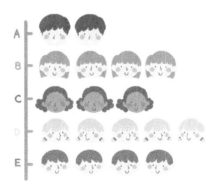

What type of art is it?

① graph

② map

③ list

Practice Test 1

Session 2

Instructions
Read each question carefully.
Each question has three answer choices.
Fill in the circle for the correct answer.

13 Emily was playing her first soccer game. Emily tried to save a goal. She missed it. The other team scored and won the match. She felt very upset. Her coach told her to keep trying.

Jake and Ryan were playing a game of basketball. Jake missed a shot and lost the game. Jake was mad at himself. Ryan told Jake not to feel bad.

How are the stories similar?

①   They are both about being a good friend.

②   They are both about losing a game.

③   They are both about learning something new.

14 The plump pig plodded through the puddles of mud.

What is used in this sentence?

①   alliteration

②   rhyme

③   simile

15 There was once a gigantic fish that lived in a lake. Every day, he swam around the lake and kept it clean. He also shared his home with other animals and protected them. He was the king of the lake.

Where does the story take place?

① an ocean

② a lake

③ a river

16 Lily was a very shy girl. She didn't like to talk to people she didn't know. One day, she had to give a speech in front of her class. She was shaking a bit, but she did a great job. Everyone was so proud.

How does Lily probably feel before giving the speech?

① excited

② calm

③ scared

17 The giraffe tried to reach the _____ leaves.

Which word completes the sentence?

   ① chew

   ② highest

   ③ hungry

18 Once there was a girl named Lily. Lily didn't like her hair because it was curly. She wished for straight hair. One day, she saw a butterfly with curly, colorful wings. She realized that being different was special. Lily became known for her special look.

What lesson does this story tell?

   ① Be yourself.

   ② Don't judge people.

   ③ Enjoy nature.

19   The fireman <u>spoke</u> to the class about his job.

What does *spoke* mean?

①   to show

②   to sing

③   to speak

20   Butterflies are flying,
Bringing us delight.
Flowers of many colors,
so lovely and so _____.

Which word goes in the blank to make an ABCB rhyme?

①   bright

②   many

③   nice

21 A mouse was afraid of the dark. She was always afraid to leave her hole. One day, she saw a cat coming. She knew she had to be brave to save her family. The mouse chased the cat away.

What is the story about?

① a mouse getting over a fear

② a mouse learning a new skill

③ a mouse making a new friend

22 Abby <u>disagreed</u> with her friend.

What does *disagreed* mean?

① did not agree

② agreed more

③ used to agree

23   Farmers grow food. They have big fields. They plant seeds in the soil. They use tractors to help them. They also take care of animals. They work hard to feed us.

What do these sentences tell?

   ①   what farmers do

   ②   how to become a farmer

   ③   why farmers work hard

24   This picture is in a text.

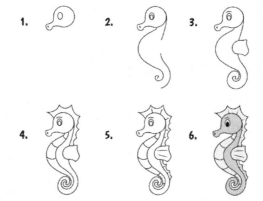

What is the text meant to do?

   ①   teach people something

   ②   make people laugh

   ③   tell people facts

Practice Test 1

Session 3

Instructions

Read each question carefully.

Each question has three answer choices.

Fill in the circle for the correct answer.

25 The sun is the star at the center of our solar system. It gives us light and heat. It also helps the plants grow. The sun is also the source of solar energy. We can use this to power our homes.

What is the author's purpose?

① to tell people why the sun is important

② to warn people that the sun is hot

③ to show that the sun will always be there

26 Olivia learned a new song. She played it on the piano. It was a piece of cake.

Which sentence uses an idiom?

① Olivia learned a new song.

② She played it on the piano.

③ It was a piece of cake.

27   Emily was walking home from school when she saw a lost puppy. She followed it until it led her to its home. The puppy's family was so happy to have their pet back.

What is Emily like?

①   playful

②   kind

③   brave

28   There once was a cat named Ted
Who loved to play with a ball of red
He'd chase it all day
Until he was done, they say
And then curl up, purring in bed.

What is the rhyme pattern?

①   AABBB

②   AABBA

③   AABBC

29 Snails move very _____.

Which word completes the sentence?

① path

② shell

③ slowly

30 Nick loved to play with his ball. He would play with it every day. One day, he learned how to do a trick shot. He couldn't wait to show everyone his new trick shot.

How does Nick feel at the end of the story?

① grumpy

② proud

③ mighty

31   The princess had a long <u>fair</u> ponytail.

Which word means about the same as *fair*?

①   strong

②   light

③   neat

32   Trees are plants. They have roots, a trunk, branches, and leaves. Trees provide us with oxygen and shade. Trees also provide homes for animals. We should take care of trees by planting more.

Which sentence gives the author's opinion?

①   They have roots, a trunk, branches, and leaves.

②   Trees provide us with oxygen and shade.

③   We should take care of trees by planting more.

33 Emily always wanted more. She never wanted to share her things. One day, she forgot her lunch. Her friend Mia gave her half of hers. Emily realized how nice it felt to share.

What does Mia share with Emily?

① her toys

② her bike

③ her lunch

34 Hannah stayed home because she was feeling <u>unwell</u>.

Which word means about the same as *unwell*?

① lonely

② sick

③ tired

35 Hot-air balloons are a fun way to travel. They float in the air with hot air inside. People sit inside the balloon and enjoy the view. They can see for miles. Hot-air balloons are an exciting way to travel.

What do the sentences tell?

①   how hot-air balloons are able to fly so high

②   where people like to travel in hot-air balloons

③   what it is like to travel by hot-air balloon

36 An article tells what Greece is like to visit. Which heading would give details about special sites to visit?

①   Enjoying the Food

②   How to Get Around

③   Famous Places

Practice Test 2

Session 1

Instructions

Read each question carefully.

Each question has three answer choices.

Fill in the circle for the correct answer.

1   We should eat more fruits and vegetables because they are
     healthy for us. They help us grow strong and give us energy. We
     will feel better if we eat them instead of junk food.

     What is the text meant to do?

     ①   inform

     ②   entertain

     ③   persuade

2   Jackson was feeling blue after losing the tennis match.

     What does "feeling blue" mean?

     ①   tired

     ②   sad

     ③   sore

3   A caterpillar named Carl was feeling sad because he couldn't fly like the birds. One day, he spun a cocoon. After a while, he turned into a beautiful butterfly. Carl was now happy and flew high into the sky.

Why is Carl sad?

① He has no friends.

② He cannot fly.

③ The birds tease him.

4   The flowers bloom,
the bees buzz by.
I love to sit under
the clear blue sky.

What is the rhyme pattern?

① AABB

② ABAB

③ ABCB

5   I wanted a snack, so I went to the _____.

① hungry

② kitchen

③ yum

6   Jack loved working on cars. One day, he saw a broken car on the side of the road. Jack wanted to help, so he found some tools and fixed the car. The owner of the car was so grateful.

What does this story have a lesson about?

① having hobbies

② helping others

③ using good manners

7 I have a <u>collection</u> of toys that I play with every day.

What does the word *collection* mean?

① a group or set

② a carton or box

③ an idea or plan

8 Space is filled with stars, planets, and galaxies. These are millions of light years away. It's filled with many wonders. Space travel is possible with the help of rockets. Scientists are always learning more. New planets are discovered all the time.

How does the author feel about exploring space?

① It is boring.

② It is exciting.

③ It is scary.

9   Exercising is good for your body. It makes you strong and helps you stay healthy. It helps you run fast and play well. It makes you feel good and gives you energy. It is fun!

What is the text about?

①   the best ways to exercise

②   how often to exercise

③   why it is good to exercise   .

10   The street looked very <u>unclean</u>.

What is the base word of *unclean*?

①   un

②   clean

③   lean

11   The beauty of Alaska is amazing. Its vast mountains are beautiful. Its slow glaciers are lovely and calming. The wildlife is like nowhere else in the world. Alaska is home to some of the most special scenery in the United States.

What is Alaska known for?

①   canyons

②   glaciers

③   volcanoes

12   The title of a text is below.

Come Along to the Seahaven Park Grand Opening

What is the text meant to do?

①   teach something

②   tell a story

③   make people do something

Practice Test 2

Session 2

Instructions

Read each question carefully.

Each question has three answer choices.

Fill in the circle for the correct answer.

13 Cats are animals. They have fur, four legs, and a tail. Cats are playful and love to cuddle. Cats can be kept as pets.

Birds have feathers, wings, and beaks. Birds can sing and build nests. Some birds can fly a long way. Birds can even fly over whole oceans.

How are the two texts similar?

① They are both about pets.

② They are both about animals.

③ They are both about flying.

14 She sang like an angel in the night.

What does this simile show about the singing?

① It sounded scary.

② It sounded quiet.

③ It sounded beautiful.

15 On a cold winter day, a group of children decided to build a snowman. They worked together to make a big snowman with a carrot for a nose and two coal buttons for eyes. The snowman made everyone smile.

When does the story take place?

① fall

② summer

③ winter

16 Sophie was always scared of trying new things. She didn't like to try anything she wasn't used to. One day, she tried a new food, and she loved it! She was so happy she tried something new.

How does Sophie probably feel before trying the food?

① calm

② excited

③ unsure

17 I stood there waiting for _____ to open the door.

Which word completes the sentence?

① knocked

② house

③ someone

18 A squirrel gathered a big pile of acorns. She was excited about eating them all. But she didn't want to eat them by herself. She offered some to the other animals. Soon, everyone was having a feast together.

What does this story have a lesson about?

① planning

② sharing

③ lying

19　Graham <u>caught</u> a huge fish.

What does *caught* mean?

  ①   to buy

  ②   to catch

  ③   to spot

20　I have a cute little cat,
Her fur is soft and warm.
She likes to play with my hat,
And purrs all through the _____.

Which word goes in the blank to make an ABAB rhyme?

  ①   house

  ②   night

  ③   storm

21   Mikey loved to swim. He would go to the pool every day. One day, he learned how to dive. He was so proud of himself. He couldn't wait to show everyone his new diving skills.

What is the story about?

①   a boy being brave

②   a boy who doesn't give up

③   a boy learning a new skill

22   The garden was very <u>untidy</u>.

What does *untidy* mean?

①   less tidy

②   very tidy

③   not tidy

23   Fish are animals that live in water. They have scales and fins. Fish have gills. These allow them to breathe when in the water. Fish are important for the environment and for food.

What allows fish to breathe?

①   fins

②   gills

③   scales

24   An article tells how to grow tomatoes. Which heading would give details about choosing the season to plant the tomatoes?

①   Watering the Plants

②   When to Plant

③   Where to Plant

Practice Test 2

Session 3

Instructions

Read each question carefully.

Each question has three answer choices.

Fill in the circle for the correct answer.

---

25 Bicycles are a fun way to ride. They have two wheels and handlebars. You pedal to make the bike move. They are good for our bodies and the environment. You should ride a bike as often as you can.

What is the author's purpose?

① to explain to people how bikes work

② to suggest that people ride more often

③ to teach people how to ride a bike

26 The twinkling stars shone brightly in the starry sky.

Which pair of words use alliteration?

① twinkling stars

② shone brightly

③ starry sky

27 A group of friends decided to go on a treasure hunt. They followed a map to a puzzle. They solved the puzzle and were given a key. They used the key to open a treasure chest.

What do the friends do first?

① follow a map

② open a chest

③ solve a puzzle

28 I see the rainbow in the sky
Its colors bright and bold and high
It's like a bridge to the other side
A promise of sunshine after a ride

What is the rhyme pattern?

① AABB

② ABAB

③ AAAA

29   Morgan listened to the rain falling on the _____.

Which word could go in the blank?

①   night

②   roof

③   storm

30   The crocodile swam in the river. It saw a mouse. It chased it all around the river. It snapped its jaws. The mouse was lucky to get away.

Who is scared in the story?

①   only the crocodile

②   only the mouse

③   the mouse and the crocodile

31 The word *break* can mean a pause or a rest. Which sentence uses the word with this meaning?

①   I was worried I could break my leg.

②   I needed a break from running.

③   I got a lucky break and won the race.

32 The Earth is a planet. It is the third planet from the Sun. The Earth has air, water, and land. The Earth is our home and we need to take care of it. People, animals, and plants all live on Earth.

Which sentence tells the author's opinion?

①   It is the third planet from the Sun.

②   The Earth is our home and we need to take care of it.

③   People, animals, and plants all live on Earth.

33 The Sun is a star. It gives us light and heat. It is the center of our solar system. The Sun is 93 million miles away from Earth. We need the Sun to live.

What is the Sun?

① a planet

② a star

③ a solar system

34 The forest was quiet and <u>peaceful</u>.

Which word means about the same as *peaceful*?

① calm

② old

③ large

35 Owls are interesting birds. They have big eyes and can turn their heads all the way around. They are good hunters and catch mice and other small animals. They are active at night and sleep during the day. Owls are beautiful and important birds.

What is the topic of the text?

①   how to spot owls

②   what makes owls interesting

③   how many types of owls there are

36 Which of these would be the title of a text with facts about camels?

①   How Do Camels Live in Deserts?

②   How to Ride a Camel

③   Carrie and her Amazing Pet Camel

Practice Test 3

Session 1

Instructions

Read each question carefully.

Each question has three answer choices.

Fill in the circle for the correct answer.

---

1 We should recycle our waste because it helps the environment. When we recycle, we keep our world clean and healthy. We can also make new things from old things.

What is the text meant to do?

① inform people about facts

② entertain with a funny story

③ persuade people to do something

2 The wobbly wagon moved like a snail along the dusty road.

Which set of words use alliteration?

① wobbly wagon

② like a snail

③ dusty road

3   A frog named Fred lived in a pond. He loved to sing and play, but he had no friends. He wanted someone to play with. One day, Fred met a turtle named Tom. They had so much fun playing and singing together, and Fred was happy that he had found a friend.

How does Fred feel at first?

① scared

② lonely

③ angry

4   I see the moon up high.
It shines so bright in the sky.
I wish I could touch and fly.
To that big ball way up high.

What is the rhyme pattern?

① AAAA

② ABAB

③ ABBA

5   I needed help to carry the _____ bags.

①   heavy

②   asked

③   move

6   A rabbit found a carrot that had fallen out of a farmer's basket. The farmer asked the rabbit if he had seen it. The rabbit told the truth, saying he had taken it. The farmer was happy and gave him another carrot as a reward.

What does this story have a lesson about?

①   being patient

②   being honest

③   being wise

7   Jay thought the movie was <u>terrible</u>, so he stopped watching it.

What does the word *terrible* mean?

①   boring

②   awful

③   long

8   Plants produce oxygen. This helps us breathe. Plants also help clean the air. People grow plants in their homes and gardens. They smell nice and make people feel good.

How does the author feel about plants?

①   They need a lot of care.

②   They are important and useful.

③   They are good gifts to give.

9   I cook food for people to eat. I use a big kitchen with many tools. I use my senses to know when the food is just right. I must work quickly to make sure everything is ready at the same time. Being a chef is busy, but fun.

What is the text about?

①   how to become a chef

②   what it is like to be a chef

③   why chefs enjoy cooking

10   You should tell the truth and not be <u>dishonest</u>.

What is the base word of *dishonest*?

①   dis

②   honest

③   nest

11 Polar bears are among the largest animals on Earth. They are found in the Arctic Ocean. They have thick fur to keep warm and a long neck for swimming long distances. They have large paws that stops them cracking the ice.

What keeps polar bears warm?

① thick fur

② long neck

③ large paws

12 The art in a text is below.

What type of art is it?

① graph

② map

③ list

Practice Test 3

Session 2

Instructions

Read each question carefully.

Each question has three answer choices.

Fill in the circle for the correct answer.

---

13   The titles of two texts are below.

How to Win at Chess

The History of Chess

How are the two texts similar?

①   They both give facts.

②   They are both about a game.

③   They both tell how to do something.

14   Jasmine was about to start her dance, but she got cold feet.

What does "got cold feet" tell about Jasmine?

①   She felt nervous.

②   She felt sick.

③   She felt excited.

15   A horse named Harry lived in a big green meadow. He loved to run and play, but he wanted to be the fastest. One day, Harry challenged all the other animals to a race. He ran as fast as he could and won the race.

What is the setting of the story?

    ①   a farm

    ②   a meadow

    ③   a zoo

16   Leah picked apples from the tree in her garden. She put them in a basket. She took them to her grandmother's house. Her grandmother gave her a hug. Then they made apple pies together.

How does the grandmother probably feel?

    ①   grateful

    ②   curious

    ③   upset

17 Last year, we went on a _____ to the snow.

Which word completes the sentence?

①　white

②　skiing

③　trip

18 A cat liked to sleep all day. She refused to help catch mice to feed the family. One day, a rat came and ate all the food. The cat realized that he needed to help. He started catching mice, and everyone was happy.

What lesson does the cat learn?

①　Don't be rude.

②　Don't be lazy.

③　Don't be greedy.

19   Harry drew a <u>rough</u> map of his house.

What does the word <u>rough</u> tell about the map?

①   It was not drawn well.

②   It was hard to draw.

③   It felt uneven and bumpy.

20   The stars twinkle in the night
They shine so bright and oh so right
I wish on them with all my might
For a dream to come true _____.

Which word goes in the blank to make an AAAA rhyme?

①   today

②   soon

③   tonight

21 Johnny often played with his toys alone. One day, he decided he wanted to play with other people. He took his toys to the park. He made a fort and invited everyone he saw to play with him. They had so much fun playing together.

What is the story about?

①   a boy learning to be kind

②   a boy being greedy

③   a boy making new friends

22 Craig was <u>hopeful</u> he would get a bike for his birthday.

What does the word *hopeful* mean?

①   had hope

②   did not hope

③   hoped more

23   Bees are very special insects. They help flowers grow by pollinating them. They also make honey. Honey is sweet and good to eat. We need to be careful not to hurt bees because they are so good to our world.

What is the main idea?

①   Bees are insects.

②   Bees are important.

③   Bees make honey.

24   This picture is in a text about Braden's first camping trip.

What does the picture help readers understand?

①   the main character

②   the setting

③   the theme

Practice Test 3

Session 3

Instructions

Read each question carefully.

Each question has three answer choices.

Fill in the circle for the correct answer.

25 Reading books is better than watching TV. You use your imagination and learn new things. You can read about different places and people. You can read about anything you want. You can learn to love reading.

What is the author's purpose?

① to explain what types of books there are

② to suggest that people read more books

③ to teach people how to choose a good book

26 The wind blew like a raging storm through the trees.

What does the simile tell about the wind?

① It was mean.

② It was strong.

③ It was cold.

27   Cameron got a new bike. He rode it down the street. He waved to his friends and they waved back. He loved riding his new bike.

How does Cameron feel?

①   happy

②   lost

③   worried

28   There once was a mouse so small
Who lived in a hole in the wall
He loved to eat cheese
With so much ease
And then sneak back, not making a call.

What is the rhyme pattern?

①   AABBB

②   AABBA

③   AABBC

29 Erin told the story from the _____.

Which word could go in the blank?

   ①   beginning

   ②   funny

   ③   listened

30 I got a new yellow dress today. I got it to wear to my birthday party. I put it on and twirled around. "Maddie, you look like a princess," my mother said. I felt so special and happy.

How do the characters feel about the dress?

   ①   Maddie and her mother both like it.

   ②   Maddie likes it, but her mother doesn't.

   ③   The mother likes it, but Maddie doesn't.

31 Beth <u>whispered</u> a secret to her friend.

What does the word *whispered* mean?

① talked quickly

② talked quietly

③ talked rudely

32 Swimming is a fun activity. People can swim in pools or in the ocean. They can swim fast or slow and do different strokes. Swimming is a good way to stay healthy and have fun. Everyone should learn how to swim.

What does the author think about swimming?

① Swimming is hard work.

② Swimming is good for you.

③ Swimming must be done safely.

33 Spiders are insects. They have two body parts and eight legs. Spiders spin webs. Spiders catch insects in their webs. Spiders come in different sizes. Spiders can be found all over the world.

How many legs do spiders have?

① two

② six

③ eight

34 The city street was very <u>noisy</u>.

Which word means about the same as *noisy*?

① busy

② loud

③ dirty

35 Ants are hard-working insects. They live in colonies and work together to find food. They can carry things that are much bigger than they are. Ants are found all over the world.

What do ants live in?

①   dens

②   hives

③   colonies

36 What would be the title of a text that tells people why bees are important?

①   The History of Bees

②   How to Keep Bees

③   Why Bees Matter

Practice Test 4

Session 1

Instructions

Read each question carefully.

Each question has three answer choices.

Fill in the circle for the correct answer.

1   A tornado is a powerful windstorm. They can cause a lot of damage. They are formed by a thunderstorm. They can happen in many different places, but they are more common in some places than others.

What is the text meant to do?

①   inform people about facts

②   entertain with a funny story

③   persuade people to do something

2   The sky lit up like a thousand candles.

What does the simile tell about the sky?

①   It was bright.

②   It was happy.

③   It was warm.

3   There was once a cat who lived in a small village. One day, a lion came to the village. The cat stepped forward and fought the lion. He saved the village from danger.

Which word describes the cat?

① brave

② funny

③ smart

4   Bunnies hopping along,
Filling us with cheer,
Kittens purring a song,
so happy and so dear.

What is the rhyme pattern?

① AABB

② ABAB

③ ABCB

5   I am going to my friend's house _____.

Which word should go in the blank?

①   fun

②   tomorrow

③   visit

6   A bird had a nest in a tree, but it was starting to get old and wobbly. The bird asked a friendly beaver to help build a new nest. The beaver was happy to help. They worked together to build a beautiful new home.

What does this story have a lesson about?

①   learning new things

②   working together

③   being strong

7   The birds are singing and <u>soaring</u> high in the sky.

What does the word *soaring* mean?

① chasing

② flying

③ screaming

8   Dogs make great pets. They can be trained to do many things. They can play fetch and learn tricks. They have many important uses. They can help people who are blind. They can herd sheep on farms.

Which detail supports the idea that dogs have important uses?

① They can play fetch.

② They can learn tricks.

③ They can herd sheep.

9 Katie didn't like to lose. When she lost a game, she would get upset. Sometimes, she would storm off. One day, she realized that nobody wanted to play with her anymore. She learned to be a better sport.

Why does Katie decide to change?

① Nobody wants to play with her anymore.

② She gets in trouble.

③ She wants to win all the time.

10 We decided to <u>rename</u> our dog Sparky.

What is the base word of *rename*?

① re

② name

③ me

11 Butterflies are insects. They have two wings and six legs. Butterflies can fly and change colors. Butterflies drink nectar from flowers. Butterflies lay eggs that turn into caterpillars.

Which sentence tells what butterflies eat?

① They have two wings and six legs.

② Butterflies can fly and change colors.

③ Butterflies drink nectar from flowers.

12 The title of a text is below.

How to Roll Sushi

What is the text meant to do?

① teach something

② tell a story

③ give facts

Practice Test 4

Session 2

Instructions

Read each question carefully.

Each question has three answer choices.

Fill in the circle for the correct answer.

13 Which text would tell how to stay safe from snakes?

① How Snakes Move About

② What to Do if You See a Snake

③ Are Snakes Good Pets?

14 The hungry hawk hovered high above the old forest.

What is used in the sentence?

① alliteration

② idiom

③ rhyme

15 One day, Mary found a secret garden hidden in her backyard. She kept it a secret and explored it every day. She discovered a magical world of plants and animals. She loved to spend time there.

What is the setting?

① a magic forest

② a secret garden

③ an old zoo

16 The puppy was lost. He barked and barked, but no one came. Then he saw a man who looked kind. "I'm William," said the man. William took the dog home and gave him a warm bed.

How does the puppy feel at the start of the story?

① angry

② brave

③ upset

17 You can _____ popcorn in the microwave.

Which word completes the sentence?

① make

② yummy

③ popping

18 Adam stood at the bottom of the rock-climbing wall. He didn't know if he could climb it. He wasn't sure if he was strong enough. But he decided to try. He took it one step at a time. He made it all the way to the top.

What lesson does this story tell?

① Believe in yourself.

② Make a plan.

③ Ask for help.

19 Anna <u>wore</u> a bright blue dress.

What does *wore* mean?

① to want

② to wear

③ to wash

20 I love to play with my toy car.
It zooms and races so far.
I always am the winner,
and then I go to _____.

Which word goes in the blank to make an AABB rhyme?

① dinner

② school

③ sleep

21 A small mouse named Max lived on a quiet farm. He wanted to see the world. He packed a bag and set out to see the world. Max saw many new sights and made many new friends.

What is the story about?

① a mouse that goes on an adventure

② a mouse that gets lost

③ a mouse that misses his home

22 The glass vase was <u>breakable</u>.

What does *breakable* mean?

① can be broken

② was broken before

③ cannot be broken

23 Baseball is a fun sport. People play it with a bat, a ball, and gloves. They try to hit the ball and score runs. Teams play against each other and try to win. Baseball is a popular sport in many countries.

Which sentence tells what is needed to play baseball?

① People play it with a bat, a ball, and gloves.

② They try to hit the ball and score runs.

③ Teams play against each other and try to win.

24 This picture is in a text.

What is the text meant to do?

① teach people something

② make people laugh

③ tell people facts

Practice Test 4

Session 3

Instructions

Read each question carefully.

Each question has three answer choices.

Fill in the circle for the correct answer.

---

25 The ocean is a special place. It is made up of different layers of water. The deepest layer is over a mile below the surface. The ocean is home to many different animals and plants. The ocean is a source of food and energy.

What is the author's purpose?

① to explain what oceans are like

② to suggest that people visit an ocean

③ to warn people to be careful in the ocean

26 Celia was on cloud nine after she won the race.

What does "on cloud nine" mean?

① very tired

② very quiet

③ very happy

27 A frog named Fred lived in a big pond. One day, Fred entered a singing contest. He sang as beautifully as he could. But he didn't win. A little bird won the contest. Fred hopped sadly back to his pond.

How does Fred feel at the end?

① proud

② excited

③ upset

28 Little Donnie loved to climb,
up tall trees all of the time.
He'd go up so high,
he didn't know why.
He'd sit up there until nighttime.

What is the rhyme pattern?

① AABBA

② AABBB

③ AABBC

29 The alarm clock buzzed early in the _____.

Which word could go in the blank?

① morning

② noisy

③ sleeping

30 The bear sat in his cave. A deer came by one day, thinking they might be friends. The bear stood up tall and roared. The deer ran quickly away and never went back.

Who feels scared in the story?

① only the bear

② only the deer

③ the bear and the deer

31 The word *left* can mean "to leave or go away." Which sentence uses the word with this meaning?

① I write with my left hand.

② I took a left turn.

③ I left the party.

32 Pennies are small coins. They are worth one cent each. People use pennies to pay for things and to save for later. Pennies have been around for a long time. It's fun to collect pennies and see how many you can save.

Which sentence gives the author's opinion?

① They are worth one cent each.

② Pennies have been around for a long time.

③ It's fun to collect pennies and see how many you can save.

33 Being a firefighter is a hard job. I help people when there are fires. I wear heavy boots and a helmet to keep me safe. I use a big hose to put out fires. I also rescue people and animals. I use a long ladder to reach high places.

What does the firefighter use to keep safe?

① helmet

② hose

③ ladder

34 James started to <u>rebuild</u> his tower of blocks.

What does *rebuild* mean?

① build again

② build more

③ not build

35   Sunflowers are beautiful flowers. They follow the sun and turn their heads to face it. They are tall and bright and can grow up to 15 feet high. Sunflowers are used to make oil and birdseed. Sunflowers are a wonderful and useful plant.

Which sentence tells what sunflowers look like?

①   They are tall and bright and can grow up to 15 feet high.

②   Sunflowers are used to make oil and birdseed.

③   Sunflowers are a wonderful and useful plant.

36   Which heading in a text gives details about when the Golden Gate Bridge was built?

①   History of the Golden Gate Bridge

②   Traffic on the Golden Gate Bridge

③   The Future of the Golden Gate Bridge

ANSWER KEY

About Florida's New English Language Arts Standards

Student learning and assessment in Florida is based on the skills listed in the new Benchmarks for Excellent Student Thinking, or B.E.S.T. The reading standards are divided into three areas: Reading Prose and Poetry, Reading Informational Text, and Reading Across Genres. The Star Reading tests also cover the skills in the Vocabulary section of the standards. The answer key that follows include the skill assessed by each question.

Practice Test 1, Session 1

Question	Answer	Skill
1	1	ELA.2.R.2.3: Explain an author's purpose in an informational text.
2	2	ELA.2.R.3.1: Identify and explain similes, idioms, and alliteration in text(s).
3	2	ELA.2.R.1.1: Identify plot structure and describe main story elements in a literary text.
4	2	ELA.2.R.1.4: Identify rhyme schemes in poems.
5	3	ELA.2.V.1.1: Use grade-level academic vocabulary appropriately in speaking and writing.
6	2	ELA.2.R.1.2: Identify and explain a theme of a literary text.
7	2	ELA.2.V.1.3: Identify and use context clues, word relationships, reference materials, and/or background knowledge to determine the meaning of unknown words.
8	3	ELA.2.R.2.4: Explain an author's opinion(s) and supporting evidence.
9	1	ELA.2.R.3.2: Retell a text to enhance comprehension.
10	2	ELA.2.V.1.2: Identify and use base words and affixes to determine the meaning of unfamiliar words in grade-level content.
11	2	ELA.2.R.2.2: Identify the central idea and relevant details in a text.
12	1	ELA.2.R.2.1: Explain how text features—including titles, headings, captions, graphs, maps, glossaries, and/or illustrations—contribute to the meaning of texts.

Practice Test 1, Session 2

Question	Answer	Skill
13	2	ELA.2.R.3.3: Compare and contrast important details presented by two texts on the same topic or theme.
14	1	ELA.2.R.3.1: Identify and explain similes, idioms, and alliteration in text(s).
15	2	ELA.2.R.1.1: Identify plot structure and describe main story elements in a literary text.
16	3	ELA.2.R.1.3: Identify different characters' perspectives in a literary text.
17	2	ELA.2.V.1.1: Use grade-level academic vocabulary appropriately in speaking and writing.
18	1	ELA.2.R.1.2: Identify and explain a theme of a literary text.
19	3	ELA.2.V.1.3: Identify and use context clues, word relationships, reference materials, and/or background knowledge to determine the meaning of unknown words.
20	1	ELA.2.R.1.4: Identify rhyme schemes in poems.
21	1	ELA.2.R.3.2: Retell a text to enhance comprehension.
22	1	ELA.2.V.1.2: Identify and use base words and affixes to determine the meaning of unfamiliar words in grade-level content.
23	1	ELA.2.R.2.2: Identify the central idea and relevant details in a text.
24	1	ELA.2.R.2.1: Explain how text features—including titles, headings, captions, graphs, maps, glossaries, and/or illustrations—contribute to the meaning of texts.

Practice Test 1, Session 3

Question	Answer	Skill
25	1	ELA.2.R.2.3: Explain an author's purpose in an informational text.
26	3	ELA.2.R.3.1: Identify and explain similes, idioms, and alliteration in text(s).
27	2	ELA.2.R.1.1: Identify plot structure and describe main story elements in a literary text.
28	3	ELA.2.R.1.4: Identify rhyme schemes in poems.
29	3	ELA.2.V.1.1: Use grade-level academic vocabulary appropriately in speaking and writing.
30	2	ELA.2.R.1.3: Identify different characters' perspectives in a literary text.
31	2	ELA.2.V.1.3: Identify and use context clues, word relationships, reference materials, and/or background knowledge to determine the meaning of unknown words.
32	3	ELA.2.R.2.4: Explain an author's opinion(s) and supporting evidence.
33	3	ELA.2.R.3.2: Retell a text to enhance comprehension.
34	2	ELA.2.V.1.2: Identify and use base words and affixes to determine the meaning of unfamiliar words in grade-level content.
35	3	ELA.2.R.2.2: Identify the central idea and relevant details in a text.
36	3	ELA.2.R.2.1: Explain how text features—including titles, headings, captions, graphs, maps, glossaries, and/or illustrations—contribute to the meaning of texts.

Practice Test 2, Session 1

Question	Answer	Skill
1	3	ELA.2.R.2.3: Explain an author's purpose in an informational text.
2	2	ELA.2.R.3.1: Identify and explain similes, idioms, and alliteration in text(s).
3	2	ELA.2.R.1.1: Identify plot structure and describe main story elements in a literary text.
4	3	ELA.2.R.1.4: Identify rhyme schemes in poems.
5	2	ELA.2.V.1.1: Use grade-level academic vocabulary appropriately in speaking and writing.
6	2	ELA.2.R.1.2: Identify and explain a theme of a literary text.
7	1	ELA.2.V.1.3: Identify and use context clues, word relationships, reference materials, and/or background knowledge to determine the meaning of unknown words.
8	2	ELA.2.R.2.4: Explain an author's opinion(s) and supporting evidence.
9	3	ELA.2.R.3.2: Retell a text to enhance comprehension.
10	2	ELA.2.V.1.2: Identify and use base words and affixes to determine the meaning of unfamiliar words in grade-level content.
11	2	ELA.2.R.2.2: Identify the central idea and relevant details in a text.
12	3	ELA.2.R.2.1: Explain how text features—including titles, headings, captions, graphs, maps, glossaries, and/or illustrations—contribute to the meaning of texts.

Practice Test 2, Session 2

Question	Answer	Skill
13	2	ELA.2.R.3.3: Compare and contrast important details presented by two texts on the same topic or theme.
14	3	ELA.2.R.3.1: Identify and explain similes, idioms, and alliteration in text(s).
15	3	ELA.2.R.1.1: Identify plot structure and describe main story elements in a literary text.
16	3	ELA.2.R.1.3: Identify different characters' perspectives in a literary text.
17	3	ELA.2.V.1.1: Use grade-level academic vocabulary appropriately in speaking and writing.
18	2	ELA.2.R.1.2: Identify and explain a theme of a literary text.
19	2	ELA.2.V.1.3: Identify and use context clues, word relationships, reference materials, and/or background knowledge to determine the meaning of unknown words.
20	3	ELA.2.R.1.4: Identify rhyme schemes in poems.
21	3	ELA.2.R.3.2: Retell a text to enhance comprehension.
22	3	ELA.2.V.1.2: Identify and use base words and affixes to determine the meaning of unfamiliar words in grade-level content.
23	2	ELA.2.R.2.2: Identify the central idea and relevant details in a text.
24	2	ELA.2.R.2.1: Explain how text features—including titles, headings, captions, graphs, maps, glossaries, and/or illustrations—contribute to the meaning of texts.

Practice Test 2, Session 3

Question	Answer	Skill
25	2	ELA.2.R.2.3: Explain an author's purpose in an informational text.
26	3	ELA.2.R.3.1: Identify and explain similes, idioms, and alliteration in text(s).
27	1	ELA.2.R.1.1: Identify plot structure and describe main story elements in a literary text.
28	1	ELA.2.R.1.4: Identify rhyme schemes in poems.
29	2	ELA.2.V.1.1: Use grade-level academic vocabulary appropriately in speaking and writing.
30	2	ELA.2.R.1.3: Identify different characters' perspectives in a literary text.
31	2	ELA.2.V.1.3: Identify and use context clues, word relationships, reference materials, and/or background knowledge to determine the meaning of unknown words.
32	2	ELA.2.R.2.4: Explain an author's opinion(s) and supporting evidence.
33	2	ELA.2.R.3.2: Retell a text to enhance comprehension.
34	1	ELA.2.V.1.2: Identify and use base words and affixes to determine the meaning of unfamiliar words in grade-level content.
35	2	ELA.2.R.2.2: Identify the central idea and relevant details in a text.
36	1	ELA.2.R.2.1: Explain how text features—including titles, headings, captions, graphs, maps, glossaries, and/or illustrations—contribute to the meaning of texts.

Practice Test 3, Session 1

Question	Answer	Skill
1	3	ELA.2.R.2.3: Explain an author's purpose in an informational text.
2	1	ELA.2.R.3.1: Identify and explain similes, idioms, and alliteration in text(s).
3	2	ELA.2.R.1.1: Identify plot structure and describe main story elements in a literary text.
4	1	ELA.2.R.1.4: Identify rhyme schemes in poems.
5	1	ELA.2.V.1.1: Use grade-level academic vocabulary appropriately in speaking and writing.
6	2	ELA.2.R.1.2: Identify and explain a theme of a literary text.
7	2	ELA.2.V.1.3: Identify and use context clues, word relationships, reference materials, and/or background knowledge to determine the meaning of unknown words.
8	2	ELA.2.R.2.4: Explain an author's opinion(s) and supporting evidence.
9	2	ELA.2.R.3.2: Retell a text to enhance comprehension.
10	2	ELA.2.V.1.2: Identify and use base words and affixes to determine the meaning of unfamiliar words in grade-level content.
11	1	ELA.2.R.2.2: Identify the central idea and relevant details in a text.
12	2	ELA.2.R.2.1: Explain how text features—including titles, headings, captions, graphs, maps, glossaries, and/or illustrations—contribute to the meaning of texts.

Practice Test 3, Session 2

Question	Answer	Skill
13	2	ELA.2.R.3.3: Compare and contrast important details presented by two texts on the same topic or theme.
14	1	ELA.2.R.3.1: Identify and explain similes, idioms, and alliteration in text(s).
15	2	ELA.2.R.1.1: Identify plot structure and describe main story elements in a literary text.
16	1	ELA.2.R.1.3: Identify different characters' perspectives in a literary text.
17	3	ELA.2.V.1.1: Use grade-level academic vocabulary appropriately in speaking and writing.
18	2	ELA.2.R.1.2: Identify and explain a theme of a literary text.
19	1	ELA.2.V.1.3: Identify and use context clues, word relationships, reference materials, and/or background knowledge to determine the meaning of unknown words.
20	3	ELA.2.R.1.4: Identify rhyme schemes in poems.
21	3	ELA.2.R.3.2: Retell a text to enhance comprehension.
22	1	ELA.2.V.1.2: Identify and use base words and affixes to determine the meaning of unfamiliar words in grade-level content.
23	2	ELA.2.R.2.2: Identify the central idea and relevant details in a text.
24	2	ELA.2.R.2.1: Explain how text features—including titles, headings, captions, graphs, maps, glossaries, and/or illustrations—contribute to the meaning of texts.

Practice Test 3, Session 3

Question	Answer	Skill
25	2	ELA.2.R.2.3: Explain an author's purpose in an informational text.
26	2	ELA.2.R.3.1: Identify and explain similes, idioms, and alliteration in text(s).
27	1	ELA.2.R.1.1: Identify plot structure and describe main story elements in a literary text.
28	2	ELA.2.R.1.4: Identify rhyme schemes in poems.
29	1	ELA.2.V.1.1: Use grade-level academic vocabulary appropriately in speaking and writing.
30	1	ELA.2.R.1.3: Identify different characters' perspectives in a literary text.
31	2	ELA.2.V.1.3: Identify and use context clues, word relationships, reference materials, and/or background knowledge to determine the meaning of unknown words.
32	2	ELA.2.R.2.4: Explain an author's opinion(s) and supporting evidence.
33	3	ELA.2.R.3.2: Retell a text to enhance comprehension.
34	2	ELA.2.V.1.2: Identify and use base words and affixes to determine the meaning of unfamiliar words in grade-level content.
35	3	ELA.2.R.2.2: Identify the central idea and relevant details in a text.
36	3	ELA.2.R.2.1: Explain how text features—including titles, headings, captions, graphs, maps, glossaries, and/or illustrations—contribute to the meaning of texts.

Practice Test 4, Session 1

Question	Answer	Skill
1	1	ELA.2.R.2.3: Explain an author's purpose in an informational text.
2	1	ELA.2.R.3.1: Identify and explain similes, idioms, and alliteration in text(s).
3	1	ELA.2.R.1.1: Identify plot structure and describe main story elements in a literary text.
4	2	ELA.2.R.1.4: Identify rhyme schemes in poems.
5	2	ELA.2.V.1.1: Use grade-level academic vocabulary appropriately in speaking and writing.
6	2	ELA.2.R.1.2: Identify and explain a theme of a literary text.
7	2	ELA.2.V.1.3: Identify and use context clues, word relationships, reference materials, and/or background knowledge to determine the meaning of unknown words.
8	3	ELA.2.R.2.4: Explain an author's opinion(s) and supporting evidence.
9	1	ELA.2.R.3.2: Retell a text to enhance comprehension.
10	2	ELA.2.V.1.2: Identify and use base words and affixes to determine the meaning of unfamiliar words in grade-level content.
11	3	ELA.2.R.2.2: Identify the central idea and relevant details in a text.
12	1	ELA.2.R.2.1: Explain how text features—including titles, headings, captions, graphs, maps, glossaries, and/or illustrations—contribute to the meaning of texts.

Practice Test 4, Session 2

Question	Answer	Skill
13	2	ELA.2.R.3.3: Compare and contrast important details presented by two texts on the same topic or theme.
14	1	ELA.2.R.3.1: Identify and explain similes, idioms, and alliteration in text(s).
15	2	ELA.2.R.1.1: Identify plot structure and describe main story elements in a literary text.
16	3	ELA.2.R.1.3: Identify different characters' perspectives in a literary text.
17	1	ELA.2.V.1.1: Use grade-level academic vocabulary appropriately in speaking and writing.
18	1	ELA.2.R.1.2: Identify and explain a theme of a literary text.
19	2	ELA.2.V.1.3: Identify and use context clues, word relationships, reference materials, and/or background knowledge to determine the meaning of unknown words.
20	1	ELA.2.R.1.4: Identify rhyme schemes in poems.
21	1	ELA.2.R.3.2: Retell a text to enhance comprehension.
22	1	ELA.2.V.1.2: Identify and use base words and affixes to determine the meaning of unfamiliar words in grade-level content.
23	1	ELA.2.R.2.2: Identify the central idea and relevant details in a text.
24	1	ELA.2.R.2.1: Explain how text features—including titles, headings, captions, graphs, maps, glossaries, and/or illustrations—contribute to the meaning of texts.

Practice Test 4, Session 3

Question	Answer	Skill
25	1	ELA.2.R.2.3: Explain an author's purpose in an informational text.
26	3	ELA.2.R.3.1: Identify and explain similes, idioms, and alliteration in text(s).
27	3	ELA.2.R.1.1: Identify plot structure and describe main story elements in a literary text.
28	1	ELA.2.R.1.4: Identify rhyme schemes in poems.
29	1	ELA.2.V.1.1: Use grade-level academic vocabulary appropriately in speaking and writing.
30	2	ELA.2.R.1.3: Identify different characters' perspectives in a literary text.
31	3	ELA.2.V.1.3: Identify and use context clues, word relationships, reference materials, and/or background knowledge to determine the meaning of unknown words.
32	3	ELA.2.R.2.4: Explain an author's opinion(s) and supporting evidence.
33	1	ELA.2.R.3.2: Retell a text to enhance comprehension.
34	1	ELA.2.V.1.2: Identify and use base words and affixes to determine the meaning of unfamiliar words in grade-level content.
35	1	ELA.2.R.2.2: Identify the central idea and relevant details in a text.
36	1	ELA.2.R.2.1: Explain how text features—including titles, headings, captions, graphs, maps, glossaries, and/or illustrations—contribute to the meaning of texts.

Made in United States
Orlando, FL
16 January 2025

57395813R00057